MIGHTY DINOSAURS

# Tyrannosaurus Rex

Aaron Carr

AV2

www.av2books.com

# AV2

## Step 1
Go to **www.av2books.com**

## Step 2
Enter this unique code

**HEDARNJUH**

## Step 3
Explore your interactive eBook!

Tyrannosaurus Rex

MIGHTY DINOSAURS

Start!

**AV2 is optimized for use on any device**

## Your interactive eBook comes with...

**Read**

**Audio**
Listen to the entire book read aloud

**Videos**
Watch informative video clips

**Weblinks**
Gain additional information for research

**Try This!**
Complete activities and hands-on experiments

**Key Words**
Study vocabulary, and complete a matching word activity

**Quizzes**
Test your knowledge

**Slideshows**
View images and captions

## View new titles and product videos at
## www.av2books.com

# Tyrannosaurus Rex

## CONTENTS

3

# Meet the Tyrannosaurus rex.

## Its name means "tyrant lizard king."

Tyrannosaurus rex was one of the largest dinosaurs that ever lived.

It was bigger than a school bus.

Tyrannosaurus rex had a huge mouth.

Its jaw was four feet long. It had 60 very sharp teeth.

Tyrannosaurus rex was a meat eater.

It could eat up to 500 pounds of meat in one bite.

# Tyrannosaurus rex had very small arms.

## Its arms were too small to help it eat.

Tyrannosaurus rex had two sharp claws on each arm.

13

# Tyrannosaurus rex used its strong legs to move quickly.

It may have been able to run more than 25 miles an hour.

**Tyrannosaurus rex lived in forests near rivers and swamps.**

It could be found
across North America.

Tyrannosaurus rex died out more than 65 million years ago.

Tyrannosaurus rex fossils formed over millions of years.

A large Tyrannosaurus rex fossil is at the Field Museum in Chicago.

People can go to museums to see fossils and learn more about the Tyrannosaurus rex.

# Tyrannosaurus Rex Facts

These pages provide detailed information that expands on the interesting facts found in the book. They are intended to be used by adults as a learning support to help young readers round out their knowledge of each amazing dinosaur or pterosaur featured in the *Mighty Dinosaurs* series.

**Pages 4–5**

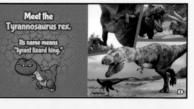

**Tyrannosaurus rex means "tyrant lizard king."** It is sometimes called T. rex. As the largest member of the tyrannosaur family of dinosaurs, T. rex was one of the fiercest predators of the prehistoric world. The T. rex is best known for its large jaw, sharp teeth, and powerful hind legs. T. rex was once thought to be the largest of all predatory dinosaurs, but larger dinosaurs, such as Spinosaurus and Giganotosaurus, have since been discovered.

**Pages 6–7**

**T. rex was one of the largest dinosaurs that ever lived.** T. rex would have been up to 21 feet (6.5 meters) tall if it had stood upright. Instead, T. rex held its body in a horizontal position, with its head forward and its tail behind for balance. T. rex could be up to 46 feet (14 m) long. It was a heavily muscled dinosaur, weighing as much as 15,000 pounds (7,000 kilograms).

**Pages 8–9**

**T. rex had a jaw that was 4 feet (1.2 m) long and had 60 sharp teeth.** The T. rex had teeth that were up to 6 inches (15 centimeters) long, or about the same size as a banana. These teeth were extremely sharp and serrated to help tear through the T. rex's food. With its huge, powerful jaw and long, sharp teeth, scientists believe a T. rex would have had a strong enough bite to tear through the roof of a car.

**Pages 10–11**

**T. rex was a carnivore, or meat eater, that could eat up to 500 pounds (230 kg) of meat in one bite.** Most scientists believe T. rex was a predatory carnivore. This means it hunted other animals for food. Fossils have shown that T. rex ate bones along with meat. Crushed Triceratops bones have been found in T. rex dung.

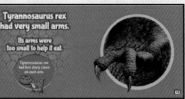

**T. rex had arms that were too small to help it eat.** The T. rex had two sharp claws on each of its two short forearms. Despite their small size, the T. rex's forearms were strong enough to hold weights up to 400 pounds (180 kg). However, the arms were likely too short to help T. rex capture or eat prey. This leads some scientists to believe that T. rex may have been a scavenger.

**T. rex may have been able to run more than 25 miles (40 kilometers) per hour.** No one is sure how fast the T. rex could run, if it could run at all. Some scientists think it could run as fast as 40 miles (70 km) per hour, though most estimates are closer to 25 miles (40 km) per hour. However, other scientists believe T. rex was too heavy to move so fast. They think it could have only managed a fast walk, like an elephant.

**T. rex lived in forests near rivers and swamps across North America.** T. rex lived in areas that had a great deal of plant life. These swamp forests had many species of trees, grasses, flowers, and other types of vegetation. Such areas attracted large plant-eating dinosaurs, such as the Triceratops and duck-billed dinosaurs. These dinosaurs were the T. rex's preferred food.

**T. rex lived more than 65 million years ago during the Late Cretaceous Period.** This period ended when a meteor impact wiped out the dinosaurs. All that people know about T. rex comes from fossils. Fossils are formed when an animal dies and is quickly covered in sand, mud, or water. This keeps the hard parts of the body, such as bones, teeth, and claws, from decomposing. The body is pressed between layers of mud and sand. Over millions of years, the layers turn into stone, and the dinosaur's bones and teeth turn into stone as well. This preserves the size and shape of the dinosaur.

**People can go to museums to see fossils and learn more about the T. rex.** Millions of people visit museums each year to see T. rex fossils in person. Many large museums, such as the American Museum of Natural History, have permanent T. rex displays. "Sue," one of the largest and best-preserved T. rex displays, is found at the Field Museum of Natural History in Chicago.

# KEY WORDS

Research has shown that as much as 65 percent of all written material published in English is made up of 300 words. These 300 words cannot be taught using pictures or learned by sounding them out. They must be recognized by sight. This book contains 56 common sight words to help young readers improve their reading fluency and comprehension. This book also teaches young readers several important content words, such as proper nouns. These words are paired with pictures to aid in learning and improve understanding.

| Page | Sight Words First Appearance | Page | Content Words First Appearance |
|---|---|---|---|
| 4 | its, means, name, the | 4 | king, lizard, Tyrannosaurus rex, tyrant |
| 7 | a, it, live, of, one, school, than, that, was | 7 | bus, dinosaurs |
| 8 | feet, four, had, long, very | 8 | jaw, mouth, teeth |
| 10 | could, eat, in, to, up | 10 | bite, meat eater, pounds |
| 12 | each, help, on, small, too, two, were | 12 | arms, claws |
| 14 | move, use | 14 | legs |
| 15 | an, been, have, may, miles, more, run | 15 | hour |
| 16 | and, near, rivers | 16 | forests, swamps |
| 17 | be, found | 17 | North America |
| 18 | out, years | 19 | fossils |
| 19 | over | 20 | Chicago, Field Museum |
| 20 | at, is, large | 21 | museums |
| 21 | about, can, go, learn, people, see | | |

Published by AV2
350 5th Avenue, 59th Floor
New York, NY 10118
Website: www.av2books.com

Printed in Guangzhou, China
1 2 3 4 5 6 7 8 9 0  24 23 22 21 20

022020
100919

Library of Congress Control Number: 2019950220

ISBN 978-1-7911-1652-1 (hardcover)
ISBN 978-1-7911-1653-8 (softcover)
ISBN 978-1-7911-1654-5 (multi-user eBook)

Project Coordinator: Priyanka Das
Art Director: Terry Paulhus

Every reasonable effort has been made to trace ownership and to obtain permission to reprint copyright material. The publishers would be pleased to have any errors or omissions brought to their attention so that they may be corrected in subsequent printings.

All illustrations by Jon Hughes, pixel-shack.com. AV2 acknowledges Alamy, iStock, and Shutterstock as its primary image suppliers for this title.